Hand-Me-Down Hannah

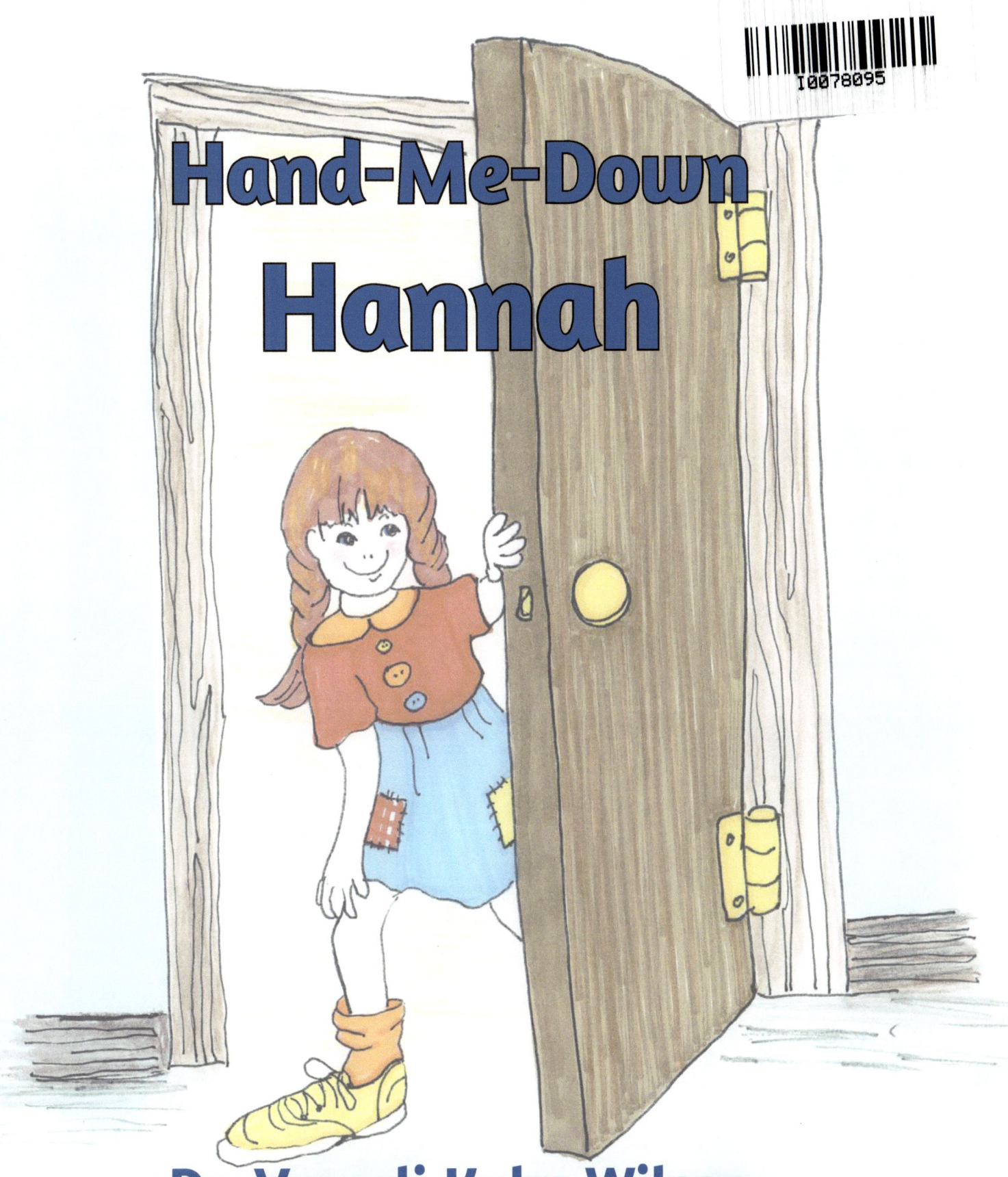

Dr. Vreneli Kuhn Wilson

Wilson Reading and Learning
La Jolla, California

Hand-me-down Hannah

Copyright 2018 by Dr. Vreneli Kuhn Wilson. All rights reserved.

For information: drvreneliwilson@aol.com

Original art by Sandra Griffith

Design and layout by Robert Goodman, Silvercat™, Encinitas, California

ISBN-13 978-0-9996653-1-2

printed in the United States of America

Hand-me-down Hannah shoes a mile too big.

Hand-me-down Hannah

a blouse too small.

Hand-me-down Hannah

a skirt too worn.

Hand-me-down Hannah

a jacket with buttons gone.

Hand-me-down Hannah

an umbrella too ripped.

Hand-me-down Hannah

a belt buckle too broken.

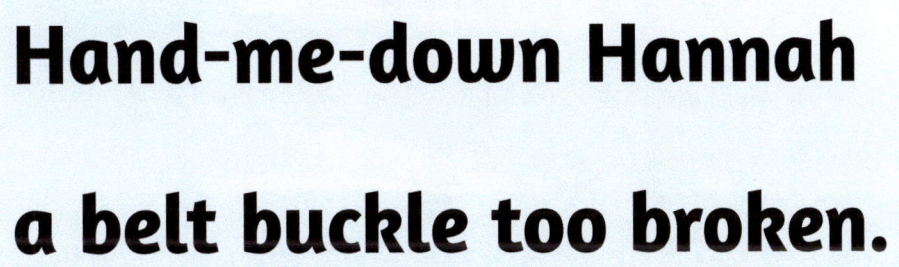

Hand-me-down Hannah

a Raggedy Ann too raggedy.

Hand-me-down Hannah

an up-side-down smile.

Hand-me-down Hannah

her birthday is today.

Hand-me-down Hannah is
Hand-me-down NO MORE.

www.ingramcontent.com/pod-product-compliance
Lightning Source LLC
Chambersburg PA
CBHW060808090426
42736CB00002B/198